CONTENTS

SMILE	4
Paris	5
Trust Me I am a doctor	6
It's YOU	7
Autumn is coming	8
Self Believe	9
Sandy Beach	10
Forgiveness	11
Without you	12
Dew Drops	13
Niagara Falls (Revisited)	14
You are strong	15
Find love again to share	16
Only with you	17
Tears are Medicine	18
Every day is fun	19
Laughter is a pill	20
You are the meaning of life	21
You dwell in my heart	23
Boats are sailing	24
Patience	25

Muteness of night	26
FINDING REAL YOU	27
Would you still Love Me????	29
Nothing to declare	30
Only you and me	31
Generation's treasure	33
Mirror	35
Tales of dual tragedy	36
Are you Okay??	38
Mermaid	40
Me and a Book	41
Taj Mahal	42
Life is a painting	43
Snow falling …	44
Happiness	45
Mum	47
Laughter	48
Solitude	49
Where is the moon gone?	50
Health Is a Gift	51
Mona Lisa	52
Autumn trees	53
Nothing beyond your reach	54
Anxious moments	55
Kaleidoscope	56
No pain no gain	57
Darkness Makes You Feel Lonely	58
Ups and downs	59
I was your last choice	60

Window shopping	61
Winter is knocking	62
Snake and Ladder	63
Beacon of hope	64
Red Apple and green tea	65
Evening Tea	66
Dew on Roses	67
A pale Blue Dot in the sky	68
Look at those eyes	69
Rain Drops	70
Joy's sorrows	71
Seasons of love	72
Lots of Roses	73
Bridges	74
Insomnia	75
About The Author	78

English Poetry & Title Page

by

Dr Nadeem Iqbal

BOOK EDITOR :SYEDA WARDA BUKHARI

This books is dedicated to all the English Lyrics & Poetry Lovers and Fans of Dr Nadeeem Iqbal

SPECIAL THANKS

To my wife ,Kidz & Mum without their help and support this book could not have been completed.

FEB 2024 UK

SMILE

SMILE

The very best gift I ever got is your smile
It's the Best of your assets in your profile

It's infectious but gone viral now
Whole world is laughing in a spiral now

Please keep it like that so I can feel all the happiness around
You are my heaven on the ground

Keep smiling and smiling my love
As its peace full and charming like Mona Lisa or above

My every day is brightened with your laughter
There is nothing better I can wish after

Dr. Nadeem Iqbal

PARIS

Under the Eiffel Tower holding hands so tight
Two hearts in Paris look one in moonlight

Gluing forces of Love, our hearts unite
A story of love written in starry night.

A melody of love spreading like a flying kiss,
In this magical night of everlasting bliss.

Blue sky above below gleaming iron grace,
Eternal city's heart, where lovers often embrace

Paris awakes with whispering secrets in the air,
Our love and the tower itself forever will be there.

Dr. Nadeem Iqbal

TRUST ME I AM A DOCTOR

Trust me I am a doctor
A little smile time to time,
Saves you from bigger disaster
Being open hearted,
Better than having open heart surgery
For all the pains and aches, you kept in locked
Though someone like me would have often knocked
But you did not respond or learnt yet
Who to believe
How to receive
But my friend it's an art
But it's an instinct as well
A gut feeling
So, listen to nobody, but your heart
And once you get the signal let go
Then see the magic
Trust yourself if not me, worth a try
You never going to know until yourself you try
If you are reading till these lines
For sure something connecting yours with mine
So have a lovely day
I wish you find you looking for your needle in the hay
Or what's best you deserve is hopefully on your way

Dr. Nadeem Iqbal

IT'S YOU

Looking for some to help you,
Look into the mirror
So now you see the right person
Remember this don't make any error

If you help yourself whole universe helps you
Unfolding wonders, believe me just for you.

So, help yourself and see the magic
All would be settled what seems tragic

This is what I have learnt so pass it to you
You say why? Because of course I LOVE YOU!

Dr. Nadeem Iqbal

AUTUMN IS COMING

Oh, my dear autumn's magic is here in the air,
Come and dance through the falling leaves with no tears.

The trees glazed in red, orange, and gold,
A story of coming months beautifully told.

So, my dear you don't feel sad but make memories here,
It's just change of a season there's nothing to fear.

Rustling dry leaves under your feet whispering
What's in your heart?
So, listen to it, if you failed once give it a new start.

Feel my shoulder just next to you
Yes, I am the sweetest voice speaking inside you.

So, dare it, hear it and once you understand
Give a big smile
Yes, be assured you are ahead completed
Another Mile though taken while

Dr. Nadeem Iqbal

SELF BELIEVE

Just believe in yourself, it can turn the skies blue,
You don't need anybody else to believe in you.

With self-respect in the soul, you can reach the stars,
In the music of life, you'll play the lead guitar

Big dreams in the pocket big hope in the eyes,
Anyone can conquer the mountains only if one tries

Life's stormy seas, would toss you around,
Keep your head up high, on solid ground.

Start believing in you then see it through,
Who else is needed to believe in you

Dr. Nadeem Iqbal

SANDY BEACH

Sitting barefooted on the sandy beach's shore
The shining sand, a canvas blank to explore,

Looking back at every step, my footprints marked the way,
Beneath the sun's warm, golden, gentle ray

Each grain beneath my soles, contains a tiny world
A tale untold, by tides and lying shells undisturbed

As waves kissed land, their secrets we unfurled
In nature's dance, a rhythm interlaced

The salty breeze caressed my flying hair
As seagulls did soar on currents high above

In this moment, I felt a sense of care
Connected to the sea, the sky, and love

I left my footprints, memories in the sparkling sand
A fleeting trace of where I chose to stand.

Dr. Nadeem Iqbal

FORGIVENESS

No one found the peace till learnt to forgive
Bitterness in you is a poison, won't let you live,

So, try Releasing the weight of grudges that you carry
In harmony, with love, and without a Worry

Let go of anger, let resentment drain
Forgiveness is the way to inner calm

By forgiving, you break the chain of pain
It brings healing like a balm

Embrace the strength to mend what's torn apart
Forgiveness is a gift you give yourself
It's not about forgetting, but about to restart

Dr. Nadeem Iqbal

WITHOUT YOU

Another sunset without you
I am again upset without you

Waves making too much noise on the beech
Looking across the sea where I am trying to reach?

There is too much quietness inside me
You are there when no one beside me

Dr. Nadeem Iqbal

DEW DROPS

Only attracts few
What's in dew?

Nothing like secret
But only if you knew

If you want to cherish moments pure and bright
Look at morning dew on roses, pure delight

On petals' canvas, tiny stars play
No one can keep eyes away

Reflecting dawn's first blush you can trace
A lovely secret kept on petals' silent space.

A fragile beauty on velvety Display
Each droplet, like a diamond shining my Way

Drop of dew, is a gift from heaven's hand,
On roses, it creates a dreamy land

Dr. Nadeem Iqbal

NIAGARA FALLS (REVISITED)

All those memories came back which I thought gone stray
Just was walking towards it just felt the sparkly spray,

Seemed to me like a kiss from nature's hand,
I was speechless at nature's artistry so grand

As I gently gazed upon glorious, majestic scene
Became everlasting memory attached to my mental screen

Water from Niagara Falls like a wall
In front of majestic beauty, I stood tall

Dr. Nadeem Iqbal

YOU ARE STRONG

In this world of endless drawbacks and tears
Often feels like all you dreamt disappears

But if you look closely then only you will see,
There's a way out to joy and set your spirit free

No matter what life brings your way,
You can gain strength to seize the day.

With a little faith and a heart open wide,
You can learn to be happy, let your light shine inside.

With just a smile on your face
Let your happiness show a pace

When darkness falls, and the night becomes long,
Tell yourself you're resilient, you are strong

Dr. Nadeem Iqbal

FIND LOVE AGAIN TO SHARE

Forgiveness is my Choice
You did what you did
Though wrong it was
Yet hatred has not seeded into my heart

From anger I'm free,
Forgiveness is my choice to heal all wounds,
Taking a fresh new start

For me hate is another burden to bear
In letting it go, I'll find love again to share

In growing hate is poisonous and blackens the day
So, smile and mend what is broken, come what may
Though we're flawed, my dear, both me and you

Dr. Nadeem Iqbal

ONLY WITH YOU

Only with you,
There's nothing I can't say or do
You are my real friend I feel it, so true

I your presence my thoughts set free
In the heat of sorrows, you are my tree

I share my dreams my secrets and my fear
A bond with you so deeply built on trust my dear

Dr. Nadeem Iqbal

TEARS ARE MEDICINE

Hidden treasures in each salty bead,
Holding the magic that broken hearts need

Numbing and soothing the wounds that time has caused
With every drop suffering is gently paused

Never shy away from tears that could fail
For in their midst, is a healing power, your call

Pearly Tears are medicine for the aching soul,
Joining the broken pieces of heart, making it pure and whole

Sliding pearls that glisten in the morning dew
They carry the power to cleanse and renew

Speaking the language of heart so aloud
Tears are a gift to help us stand tall and be proud

Dr. Nadeem Iqbal

EVERY DAY IS FUN

I love to dance under the stars all night
Continue to be happy next day in sunlight

I chase my passions and follow my dream
Unfolding my creativity in its full stream

I laugh a loud until my lungs are sore,
Living my life to the fullest but wanting more

I am grateful for the blessings I receive,
And spread kindness wherever I believe

Don't just live an easy life, you and I,
With open hearts and keep spirits high,

Embracing joy, love, and every day is fun,
Living fully, until our days are finally done.

Dr. Nadeem Iqbal

LAUGHTER IS A PILL

Laughter is a pill
That makes you often chill

The pain gets killed
And Happiness refilled

Laughter is the best medicine
It's free can be found within

So, let's laugh more and more
It's the best thing hearts adore

Keep smiling makes you strong
A cure that lasts life long

Believe me or not,

Laughter is a contagious thing
A joy that makes my sprit sing

Dr. Nadeem Iqbal

YOU ARE THE MEANING OF LIFE

When I open my eyes in the morning
I see the glow of the Sun in your eyes
When I close my eyes in the night
You shine like stars over the skies

That's the best feeling of life....
You are the meaning of life...
Yes, you are... oh baby

Never surrender whatever does happen
Holding my hands together in heaven
Keep smiling till I die
We shall have strongest of the ties

That's the best feeling of life....
You are the meaning of life...
Yes, you are... oh baby

Those blue eyes
In which reflect seven skies
You are my treasure to be
You are my pleasure to be
Never say never say
Never say goodbye

That's the best feeling of life....
You are the meaning of life...
Yes, you are... oh baby

SMILE

YOU DWELL IN MY HEART

Drops in the ocean stars on the sky
Blue birds flying over the mountain
Dancing n jumping Deers in the jungle

You dwell in my heart
You dwell in my heart
You live in my soul we can't be apart

Fallen leaves of autumn trees
Setting you and me free
Burning flames of unknown desire
Turning the golden dust into fire
Why not to-gather holding hands we fly
Over the blue sky

Singing the sonnet of a cuckoo bird
Building the new nest to take the rest
You dwell in my heart
You dwell in my heart

Dr. Nadeem Iqbal

BOATS ARE SAILING

Boats are sailing, Albatross flying
Me sitting by the bay, enjoying
Not so much deep, water Kids even tackle the waves
Shells swept across the sand
Shining star, every grain Sky blue above shines

Sun smiling too, much often
What a day it has become
Some needed the shade even
Some bare feet walked miles
Here comes the pigeon again
Picking some leftover from me lunch
Though I licked every bit of the flavour
What a day it's been,
I love the heat, then cool breeze

What a scene
What I have felt
What I have seen.

PATIENCE

Worried and always rushing. You forget the golden rule,
Yes, patience is a virtue, it can be your greatest tool.

If you are calm, you see your strength, your steady line
Being patient is an art, so rare and fine

If mastered, it's a shield against any tough call
No storm can stop you no obstacle no wall

Facing life's trials, we learn to comprehend
With patience, mountains move and oceans bend

In stillness, I discovered my true might
My patience to me like a beacon in the night,

With a heart that's full of hope your spirit strong and still,
Conquer any challenge as patience is your skill

When situation feels hasty, and impatience takes its toll,
Remember, my dear friend, patience is a skill within your soul.

Dr. Nadeem Iqbal

MUTENESS OF NIGHT

In the muteness of night,
World is bathed in silver light

Without you can't find peace and grace.
Feeling so lonely in this chaotic space.

Thought of you enchants me from dusk to dawn
I am in middle of nowhere, withdrawn

Like a never-ending symphony plays
Wind blows and sings sweetly and sways

Dr. Nadeem Iqbal

FINDING REAL YOU

By simply just worrying nothing is gain
And if I don't do anything what a pain

If I don't take the risk, I would never know,
True you, a smile that brightly tends to show

The heart's desire, a chance I must embrace,
To find the truth about love that time cannot erase.

In fear of what may happen if I try, or I do shy
But can miss the joy that's found beneath your sky

So let me take the leap, with no more delay,
To glimpse the truth in every smile you display
For in the daring dance of love's ballet,
Our hearts combined emotions on display.

True you, kept hidden in the shadows deep,
Like a puzzle with many secrets to keep.

So how can I unearth your genuine face?
In this enigma, I am lost to find my place.
Gentle exploring, I'll seek your hidden core,

SMILE

Trying to explore layers to discover more.

With empathy and time, I'll navigate,
You hide all secrets, you always hesitate.

But in the end, I hope to understand,
The real you, held within your own hand.
For in the shadows, mysteries may brew,
Yet, I'll continue to persist in finding the real you.

So, you wonder why I want to do that Answer is simple
I want to discover reason for actual pain
Behind your smiley face with a dimple,

To be continued...

Though you are laughing
But why feels like you are hiding something, or you are in pain
So please be sure I am not stranger, just explain

True you, hidden in shadows of soft embrace,
A mystery I do not want long to truly face.

In depths obscure, your essence lies concealed,
But me trying to find the real you, the truth revealed.

Taking gentle steps with subtle grace,
I'll search with care, your inner self to trace.

No hurry or rush for time will surely tell,
The secrets of the heart, where stories dwell.

With open heart and eyes that keenly see,
Let real you emerge, be clear and free
In shadows' dance, our souls would be defined
And through this journey, your true self I'll find.

WOULD YOU STILL LOVE ME????

Would you still love me if I have nothing left?
But in my hand, a bunch roses deftly kept
No fame, no million followers to behold,
With a humble gesture my love's story to be told
No fortune's treasure, no financial acclaim
With gentle breeze I'll blow on love's bright flame
Yet in my heart, a love that's pure and true
A simple gift, my heart opened bare for you.
For fame and riches, they may come and go
But love enduring, like these blooms so fair
In poverty or plenty, let it show
Our love, a bond no riches can compare
So, answer me, my love, without a doubt
Without fame, my heart's yours throughout.
Would you still love me with no fame?
Without million followers to sing my name
But in my heart is a treasure more than gold.
A love so true, it never could grow old
For me in humble gifts, love finds its way
In flowers' fragrant beauty, come what may
And fame and fortune can't replace its worth
Our love grows on, the sweetest gift on Earth
So, would you still love me, just as I am?
And you be just like you that's the aim

Dr. Nadeem Iqbal

NOTHING TO DECLARE

Don't you recognise me now?
Only have just lost my accounts and fame
But did not lose my hope, my courage, my name

But you have surely changed now
But as I was, I am surely the same
Learning still to come back to surface
Needs my heart to tame

It's not easy to be always positive
But I would try my best and that's the Game
I am what I am, and I take it
It's no shame
I am clear Nothing to declare, No one to blame

Dr. Nadeem Iqbal

ONLY YOU AND ME

But only you and me
Don't say a word
Don't say a thing
Nothing needs saying
Nothing needs listening
I hear your whispers
You can read my Mind
Time has frozen
Just in this moment
Moment is ours
Moment is divine
There is no one else
But only u n me
There is only you, there is only me
How deep and how gentle
Shades are over the sky
Dancing clouds over the hills
You been never so shy
The Time has frozen
Just in this moment
Moment is ours
Moment is divine
There is no one else
But only you and me
Fragrance of your presence
Taken all over me
One glance of yours
Casting spell on me
Melting my heart like a candle

And in this moment
No one else is there
But only there is you, but only there is me

Dr. Nadeem Iqbal

GENERATION'S TREASURE

Let's share some passion in an ageless song,
In a laughter with tears how we belong.
Lessons passed of courage and how to shine,
Generations' treasures are truly divine

Aging hands direct the young hearts' flight,
Hinting futures with insight so bright
Experiences whispered, like stars in the night,
Generations' constellation, shiny and bright

Ancestral voices in stories   merely join
In time's tapestry millions of threads entwine,

With joy and trust and prayers combine
It would be yours once it was mine
Those connections that generations create.
In family's circle, love always resonates.

Grandpa's tales, woven with dare
Pouring secrets, new lessons to share.
With hands wrinkled by years,
Still guiding us both in joys and tears.

Parental bridge between young and old,
Glowing hearts, humble but bold
A dance of knowledge, hand in hand join
The circle complete, as new stars brightly shine

Previous sacrifices show a love so pure,

A legacy of care that will always endure.
Young ones, keen with wide eyes with a glow
Learn from the past, as they bloom and grow

Dr. Nadeem Iqbal

MIRROR

All the secrets and tales untold,
In front of a mirror only truths unfold

Eyes when engage in intimate embrace.
No reluctance finds its space

The cloak of lonely souls is swiftly torn
In front of you your clone is born

Yet mirrors hold reflections, unafraid
You hear those words dare never Said

Images bear witness to anguish and despair,
They reach out to the heart seldom wounds repair.

One only can see, never can touch
It's so beautiful yet beautiful as such

Mirror so deep as deep as heart
But keeps unseen wall to keep you apart

Dr. Nadeem Iqbal

TALES OF DUAL TRAGEDY

Intertwined, forever tales of dual tragedy
In icy depths, they all sleep together quietly

Then Titanic, mighty vessel, thought unsinkable
Ocean gate with all modern tech imploded unbelievable

So, it proves that when and where fate is written
One is Lured to the spot right within
Below the waves, where light dare not intrude
Magnet for Dreams and unfilled wishes protrude

Sucking all who are keen to find centre of gravity
Lost their entity but found now new identity

They went where echos lose their sound
The only flight was inbound
Two tragedies entangled forever, no one found
Human triumphs lost, where hopes were drowned

Let their stories serve as beacons of grace,
To guide us through the tempest's darkest hour

And in remembrance, let us find a place
In our hearts where lives their Memory
Their faces their voices their every Trace

A crew of brave souls ventured to explore
Their disappearance, a key to knowledge's door.

For each soul lost regardless of their state

Let's remember them all who met their fate.

Dr. Nadeem Iqbal

ARE YOU OKAY??

Are you ok? A tender question whispered
In three words a lifeline offered
In darkness, when all things creep
A gentle touch, a kind concern can run so deep,

To a burdened heart weary, worn, and sore,
Creating hope, spirit as new to restore.
Merely connected by threads of empathy,
Be a beacon shining through adversity.

In these words, a power lies untamed,
To heal, to mend, to make you understand

So, when you hear words, "Are you okay?"
Let not your pride or fear keep truth away.
Embrace my caring soul that crosses your way,
And let my smile help brighten up your day.

For in this simple phrase, a real gift resides,
A bridge between two hearts, a safe confide.
With open arms, just free healing I can provide,
True haven where your burdens can subside.
It's you to choose, you decide
You hold my hand and take the ride

So, let me ask you again with genuine concern,
And listen to the answers as they honestly turn,
For in our unity, we all can learn,
Take a new road from this turn.
By just asking are you okay? Let's make this world a place,
Where live kindness love and praise.

Inquiring minds, compassion will embrace,
Could heal the wounds you thought one couldn't face.

Dr. Nadeem Iqbal

MERMAID

Under the waves a vision comes to sight
A maiden crowned with Jewells shiny and bright

Though it's my fantasy but can captivate you too
Because thought of her siren eyes can mesmerise is true

A creature with skin of gold and glistening hue,
With mystic charm and beauty that pursue

Around her neck are pearls and corals so delicate
That fills every heart with pure etiquette

A lovely fantasy not everybody can find
A myth that still captivates the human mind

A wondrous tale of magic, lovely mermaid in flash
All other beauties in front of her like Trash

Although she captivates with her illusion,
She's but a dream a fleeting exclusion

Do not let your heart a bit swept away
In spite she tempts with all her beauty on display

Dr. Nadeem Iqbal

ME AND A BOOK

Book is still a best friend
Though No one follows, it's a gone Trend

I Hold it, open it, read it and enjoy
Opening the pages what a fun o Boy

See what adventures one can find inside
While having tea and listening to music in a stride

When I was a kid liked
A cat inside a hat, or a mouse in the house
A bear on the chair and a frog that bounce
But now I like some grown up stuff
A love affair or a laughing killer clown
A good story which becomes Talk of the town

In a book there are so many friends to meet,
In every story there is a new world to greet.

Don't just regret why so long it took
Just find a moment and curl up with a book

Every single page you turn and a new word you say,
Learn and grow in a wonderful way

Dr. Nadeem Iqbal

TAJ MAHAL

White marble and gardens green
Behold your sight a wonder to be seen

By banks of the Yamuna River
Stands with splendour makes me shiver

Symbol of love and devotion
Full of joy a sight of emotion

Built by a king for his queen
A promise of love, forever to be seen

Intricate carvings with precious stones
Symbol of love in heart blood and bones

Domed roof, minarets tall
Visual treat for one and all

Taj Mahal, a beauty so rare
I love you so much beyond compare

Dr. Nadeem Iqbal

LIFE IS A PAINTING

Life is a painting, too personal, an intricate piece
Filled with colours, emotions, and memories to release

A canvas on which I have and would create my own design
A masterpiece that's unique, only and only mine

With every stroke, I have added another layer,
Shades of joy, sorrow, love, and despair

Have painted my dreams and unknown fears,
All my achievements, failures, and of course tears.

The canvas is vast, but the time is very short,
So, every day is a brushstroke, a new cohort

A chance to create something magical,
To make our lives meaningful and beautiful.

So only paint your life with care,
With passion, love. And be fair

To the story of your life so much you contribute
So let your canvas be a lovely memorable tribute

Dr. Nadeem Iqbal

SNOW FALLING ...

Ground is covered in pure white,
Magical! What a glorious sight

Look how softly gently floating by
Tiny Snowflakes falling from the sky,

Some Building snowmen, having fun,
Some Making snowballs one by one,

Gliding Slipping, tripping Round
Like Amazing slops in wonderland found.

Snowflakes settling everywhere so fair
Light coming through the chilly air,

Peaks of the hill are already crowned
Winter's blanket is on the ground

Don't you want to hold hands and go?
Dancing madly in the falling snow

Laughing, playing, filled with glee,
Feeling so warm though it's so chilly

Dr. Nadeem Iqbal

HAPPINESS

To be happy is not an easy feat,
But if one tries it can be sweet.

Try to learn to cherish the little things,
Listen to birds see the joy they bring

Sense the warmth of sunshine on the skin,
Or the laughter of a loved one, with a grin.
Try to count your blessings each day,
And let gratitude guide you the way,
A thankful heart is a happy heart,
In it for every moment, there's a fresh start.
Just let go all. Of your worries and fears,
Are you ready to face each challenge with courage and cheers?
If you feel life is an adventure, not a test,
Live with a positive mindset, you are blessed.

Keep surrounded yourself with love
From family, friends, and the ones above,
For a life without love is empty and frozen cold,
But with love, your heart can actually unfold.
Do pursue your passions and real dreams,
And let your soul fly with vibrant lovely beams,
For when you do what you love with zeal,
Happiness is yours to feel, it's a Deal.
So, my dear friends take these tips to heart,
And let them be your guide from the start

For a happy life is within your own reach,
And with joy and love, it's yours to teach

Dr. Nadeem Iqbal

MUM

You were there from the very start,
Holding me close to your chest safe in your heart

Guiding me through the ups and downs,
Helping me grow and never letting me drown.

All the smiles you have brought my way
For every one of those tears, you wiped away

You sacrificed so much to give me the best,
Working hard day and night never taking rest

Always been there to lend an ear and hand,
Teaching me to stand tall and take a stand.

For every hug that I have received
Thanks for every prayer since I was conceived

I know for well I can never repay you,
For all that you've done and all that you do

And for every dream that you helped me see
I am Grateful for every word that you said for me,

I hope these lines I have written will show you,
Just how much I love and appreciate you.

And I thank God to have you every single day,
I appreciate and thank you for being my mum every day

Dr. Nadeem Iqbal

LAUGHTER

Your Laughter is a precious thing,
Your smile makes me sing

Your fragrance spreads like wildfire all around,
You are a symphony of happiness unbound.

Presence of you brightens up the day,
And takes my every care away.

You are a medicine for my soul,
A healing balm that plays a role

I smile too as expression of joy
A celebration that no one can destroy

So let us laugh together with all our might,
And let it show its pure delight.

For in this world of sorrow and pain,
Your Laughter is a gift I must sustain.

Dr. Nadeem Iqbal

SOLITUDE

Stillness of the night
Look what it creates
Dancing moonlight
On clouds like waves
Shiny reflections and dark silhouettes
Eyes just wonder over the Gates

In the courtyard I am standing bare footed
Though its little cold so little gutted
Moon is bright shining and casting a spell
I called you a name but can't spell
A melody that night plays
Memory of you that never fades

In the muteness of night,
World is bathed in silver light
Without you can't find peace and grace.
Feeling so lonely in this chaotic space.

Thought of you enchants me from dusk to dawn
I am in middle of nowhere, withdrawn
Like a never-ending symphony plays
Wind blows and sings sweetly and sways

Dr. Nadeem Iqbal

WHERE IS THE MOON GONE?

Where is the moon gone?
In the midnight's clouds where is the moon gone.
After you departed, soon as soon gone

Its shiny face, like a mirror to my heart
Now vanished in the vastness, drifting apart.

Once it danced with your laughter
But like you, it also vanished after

In the silence of night, looking for its grace,
In the hopes of finding your lasting trace.

Though the moon may hide in the ocean waves
And you've faded too like a light inside a cave

I'll keep the images of your presence, dear,
In the frames of my heart, forever clear

For even when you and the moon are gone,
In the tapestry of stars, our love still on

And as dawn awakens, I have written many new day's songs
With the hope I'll find you again where the moon belongs.

Dr. Nadeem Iqbal

HEALTH IS A GIFT

Rise above your couch or chair don't just sit there
Health is a gift let's breath in some fresh air

Ever tried on two wheels when you pedal through the day,
The wind kissing your face like a mum along the way.

Make open road, your canvas, wide and grand,
Either jog or bike, make fitness your stand

Dr. Nadeem Iqbal

MONA LISA

In every stroke million tales unfold
Mona Lisa's smile, still a story untold.

Just a smile but with such a grace,
In every gallery, she finds top place.

With her following gaze no matter where one stands
It's a masterpiece a treasure that forever expands

Mona Lisa smiling forever in my sight,
Making my day brighter with all her light.

Her expression no one can replace
Nothing can fade her impressions laid.

Dr. Nadeem Iqbal

AUTUMN TREES

Within every whisper of the lovely breeze
Within every rustling of the autumn trees

I felt your presence, though you're far away
In seeking you, I found myself each day

I have lost myself in the race of finding you
I've lost myself, pursuing dreams of you
Give shadows cast by love 'Through winding paths I pursue
Myself in fragments, I discover now what is true

I could not find the strength to keep you in my sight.
Though lost, I'll never cease to chase your light
For in your presence, everything feels right
Waiting till you say you are mine with delight

This race makes me tire, but hope will not grow dim
As long as I'm consumed by thoughts so firm

With every stride, I feel our souls align
In finding you, I've found love is Devine

So, in this race, I have never counted the cost
For in your love, the best prize my heart is truly lost.

NOTHING BEYOND YOUR REACH

With every trial, every twist and bend,
Have you not found strength yet my friend?

Using passion as your guide and love as your clue,
There's nothing beyond your reach you can't do

Dr. Nadeem Iqbal

ANXIOUS MOMENTS

If anxious moments and fears grip your heart
Don't. Ever let your worries tear you apart

When all the world seems dark and dire
Fight it back with your spirit to aspire

Dr. Nadeem Iqbal

KALEIDOSCOPE

Through shattered fragments but seem to closely blend
My life's a tapestry with no loose end

Like a kaleidoscope, in every turn
Always New pattern always new colour, so much to learn

Dr. Nadeem Iqbal

NO PAIN NO GAIN

No pain, no gain, you heard again and again
With every upset, some lessons we gain

That's the best part of any Turmoil and pain
So don't you worry about any droughts it brings
All sorrows to be washed it's going to Rain

Dr. Nadeem Iqbal

DARKNESS MAKES YOU FEEL LONELY

When the day is obscured by the melancholy
Do not let the darkness make you feel lonely

If the joy seems lost and beyond your reach
Don't just still idle take a walk on the beech

Don't be lost and lean backwards
But find a way to heal and move forward

Dr. Nadeem Iqbal

UPS AND DOWNS

Lives like a ride with ups and downs
Begins from birth until you are underground

It's full of choices, and has consequences one face
So, find a purpose, and run your own race

Dr. Nadeem Iqbal

I WAS YOUR LAST CHOICE

You were mine first
And I was your last choice
Even if you said No
At least you listened, it was nice

I may not find you but
You know where always I could be found

As a high flyer you must look down upon me
I would keep my feet always on the ground

Dr. Nadeem Iqbal

WINDOW SHOPPING

Window shopping, a soothing remedy
Are you? But I am always ready
Through shiny glass, glance of treasures I desire
A moment's respite from life's troubles entire

In each display, a fantasy is brought to life
Talking to even a manikin, seen my own wife

No need for purchase, just the act of its own
A therapy for weary souls, a pleasure ingrown

So, pop often into every
New or old retail shrine

From window to window
It's wonderfully divine
Telling you the truth
Pleasure is mine

Dr. Nadeem Iqbal

WINTER IS KNOCKING

Winter just knocking on my door
My feet can sense now cooler floor

Waiting for dancing snowflake's delicate ballet
Painting with a brush in one hand and in other a colour pallet

So, l am waiting for snow with patient heart,
For in its beauty is hidden nature's perfect art

Dr. Nadeem Iqbal

SNAKE AND LADDER

Life to me is like a game of snake and ladder
Happier at times or even sadder

I have set my sight on distant, elusive goal
Neglecting desire that lives in my soul

My life is just like burning oil
Drop by drop it's taking away my turmoil

This is how grief is compounded by grief
Like a cocktail with taste of a new poison in brief

I am the main target
Of Desires which I neglected
I know this all self-educated
My soul is now like an innocent prisoner
And my body is like a Jail
How can you? I could not even find my own trail

I have committed crime of love, and all the lawyers disown
And now everybody is a judge with no mercy shown

BEACON OF HOPE

Your smile is a present costing nothing to give,
But really means everything for one who receive,

Your smiley face like a beacon of hope in a stormy sea,
Golden ray of light in the darkness, setting me free.

Dr. Nadeem Iqbal

RED APPLE AND GREEN TEA

Upon a cozy hand knitted rug, embraced by threads
Savouring moments where time softly treads.

Absorbing the soft glow of the afternoon sun,
With a cup of green tea, my daily ritual begun

Red apple's sweetness, crisp delight,
A duet of flavours, a tranquil in sight

Sipping tranquillity from the tea's green stream,
A symphony of flavours, like a peaceful dream.

In hand, a red apple like colour of your lips
On a cozy rug,
Where moments of past and future come and hug

Remembering your whispers Nadeem sweet and bold,
With harmony of tastes a new story to be told.

Dr. Nadeem Iqbal

EVENING TEA

Your smiling face and a sip of evening tea
In my window Sun is shining by the sea

With cups in hands, looking at each other
Every smile of yours looks better than the other

Dr. Nadeem Iqbal

DEW ON ROSES

If you want to cherish moments pure and bright
Look at morning dew on roses, pure delight

On petals' canvas, tiny stars play
No one can keep eyes away

A fragile beauty on velvety Display
Each droplet, like a diamond shining on my Way

Dr. Nadeem Iqbal

A PALE BLUE DOT IN THE SKY

A pale Blue Dot in the sky
Have seen the pictures of the earth somewhere
Every place, person I have ever known
Resides in that dot but why?
Only one knows
Is the One who could have made it with Joy?
So, it's seems The Universe itself
Is nothing but just a scene to enjoy?
Giant after giant
Even bigger than ever before seen
Or few even bigger one to come yet never seen before
We been struggling hard
To see hear or find aliens
But failed to see so many within
Hearted, poverty, racism and negligence
Just few on the tip of iceberg
Time is flying or running out for many
But enjoy your flight while onboard

Dr. Nadeem Iqbal

LOOK AT THOSE EYES

Look at those eyes, pleasant surprise
I am frozen when you smile

Take me with you, wherever you go
Holding your hands only desire

There is no choice out of love
For me there is nothing else but you

Imagine hard
Together in the yard of the temple of love
Dreams have come true
You only have to believe in me once
Rest is magic, magic of love

Petals of Love, Sprinkle the way
Feeling your fragrance from Miles away

Feeling the beat, deep in the heave
Linking together all chains of command
Holding your hands feeling not hurt No pain
I don't know what to say can't explain

RAIN DROPS

Each droplet playing a note on my skin
So cold it seems but warmth lies within

A melody of moments, pure and warm
Like your lovely smile with your charm

For in this rain, a love so pure and true,
I cherish each drop every moment with you.

So let the cold surround me, I'll endure,
For in that rain, our love remains so pure.

All of that washed away the pain
Rain stopped but warmth remains,

Now drenched in memories, a tale unfolds,
In rain, love's story, forever holds

Dr. Nadeem Iqbal

JOY'S SORROWS

Joys Sorrows
Silence Screams
Any buyers?
Selling my dreams

Fulfilment to be achieved
But only by not to get
What you wanted
But instead
To live with a smile
Without what you wanted

Intolerance would make you pay
With Your peace and your heart
If you don't learn to be patient
You can't stay be ready to depart

Dr. Nadeem Iqbal

SEASONS OF LOVE

Waves of the oceans
Can do me no harm
Holding just your hands
Keeping me warm

Come winter, summer
Autumn or spring
But season of love
No one can bring

So keep the windows
Of your eyes
And door of your heart open

You might find
What you been
Looking for
It might happen

And once you have
What you wished
Always be grateful
So it never diminished
Stay close to love
Give hugs and kisses
As once it's gone
One always misses

Dr Nadeem Iqbal

LOTS OF ROSES

Lots of Roses
Red and Pink
I am loving it
What you think

Putting in the vase
One by one
All my treasures
Leaving none
Happiness radiates all around
Feeling like a King I am crowned

So keep pouring your fragrance
Upon me till I last
Pleasure is all mine
So loud like a blast

Never satay away
Never waste a moment
As our time spent together
In more than important

Dr. Nadeem Iqbal

BRIDGES

All those bridges
Though I have crossed
But here I am
Back again where I was

How many fulfilments
Really needs to be fulfilled
To feel really happy
How much I have to be grilled

Dr. Nadeem Iqbal

INSOMNIA

Tired now of blinking
Still awake
Could not close the shutters of vision
Still ablaze under closed eyes
Flashes of yesterday
Like fire crackers
Noises of all hear say still
Seeking my attention
Such a loud silence
Has shattered capacity
Of my audition
So how could I get over this?
To reach stillness
Have tried taking mind off
But again was thrown back
On the same spot
Same time
Same place
So have to still figure it out
How to feel cool
Not to make myself fool
I am looking for a black hole
So can get myself absorbed
So, I can soon find myself on the other side
To meet and greet
Real me.

DR NADEEM IQBAL

SMILE

For More Poetry By Dr Nadeem Iqbal

Please Follow The Page On Facebook

https://www.facebook.com/profile.php?id=100090601996029

ABOUT THE AUTHOR

Dr Nadeem Iqbal

MRCGP UK
DRCOG
DFSRH
DGM

DR NADEEM IQBAL is a Poet ,Lyricist ,Vocalist and Music composer & Calligrapher .

Printed in Dunstable, United Kingdom

74616022R00047